I0108761

GOSPEL FOUNDATIONS
NEW BELIEVER'S CLASS

Gospel Foundations New Believer's Class
Copyright © Michael Down 2020.

Scripture quotations are from The ESV® Bible (The Holy Bible, English Standard Version®), copyright © 2001 by Crossway, a publishing ministry of Good News Publishers. Used by permission. All rights reserved.

If you cannot afford to purchase additional copies of this workbook, or need them in a hurry, you are free to photocopy any part or all of this publication, as long as you include this page. If you are a church wishing to print multiple copies for your ministry, please contact me for permission and the printable pdf.

If you have been helped by this resource, have any questions, or would like to get in touch for any other reason, I can be reached at www.michaeldown.ca.

Contents

SESSION 1:
WHAT IS THE BIBLE?

It is appropriate that we begin our investigation of Christianity with the text that is the authority in all matters of Christian belief. The Bible is a lamp to our feet and the whole of our study will look to it.

WHAT KIND OF WRITINGS MAKE UP THE BIBLE?

The Bible is a collection of books that tell the story of God and His interactions with people. It contains two testaments. THE OLD TESTAMENT begins with Genesis, describing the creation of the world, the "fall" of mankind into sin and the work of God in choosing Abraham and his offspring as His chosen people – people to be spared the judgment that would come to the rest of the world for their sin. The rest of the books of law describe the law that was given to God's people (the Israelites), so that they might pay for their sin and earn a right standing with God. We then learn about the history of God's people trying to (quite unsuccessfully) put the law into practice. The books of poetry then record different people's interactions with God and others in a more artistic, emotive way – praise, lament, despair, hope, love, hate – the whole breadth of human emotion. Finally in the Old Testament the books of prophesy record God sending prophets to try to correct the errors of His people, and to tell of a saviour yet to come.

	LAW	HISTORY		POETRY	MAJOR PROPHETS	MINOR PROPHETS	
OLD TESTAMENT	Genesis Exodus Leviticus Numbers Deuteronomy	Joshua Judges Ruth 1 Samuel 2 Samuel 1 Kings	2 Kings 1 Chronicles 2 Chronicles Ezra Nehemiah Esther	Job Psalms Proverbs Ecclesiastes Song of Songs	Isaiah Jeremiah Lamentations Ezekiel Daniel	Hosea Joel Amos Obadiah Jonah Micah	Nahum Habakkuk Zephaniah Haggai Zechariah Malachi
	GOSPELS	**HISTORY**	**LETTERS**				**PROPHESY**
NEW TESTAMENT	Mathew Mark Luke John	Acts	Romans 1 Corinthians 2 Corinthians Galatians Ephesians	Philippians 2 Colossians 1 Thessalonians 2 Thessalonians 1 Timothy	2 Timothy Titus Philemon Hebrews James	1 Peter 2 Peter 1 John 2 John 3 John / Jude	Revelation

THE NEW TESTAMENT begins with four gospels that give the account of this saviour, Jesus, and His birth, ministry, death and resurrection, followed by one book, Acts, that records the very early history of the Church as they proclaim the gospel and invite all people to join the people of God by repenting of their sin and putting their trust in Christ. Most of the rest of the New Testament is letters written by the apostles to different Churches and Christians with instructions on how to live as a Christian. Finally, the book of Revelation is a book of prophesy, mostly about things yet to happen. These are the books of the Bible, within each book you will see big numbers that indicate the chapters (usually about a page long) and small numbers that indicate verses (usually a sentence or two). So a reference such as Luke 2:15 means the fifteenth verse of the second chapter of the book of Luke.

WAS THE BIBLE WRITTEN BY GOD?

Yes. While Christians have differing views about the exact nature of Scripture, Christians have classically believed that the primary author of the Bible is God. It was human beings that put pen to paper, but God, in His sovereignty, inspired them to write exactly what He meant them to – even if they didn't realize it! Christians have therefore historically believed five things about the nature of Scripture. First, that it is inerrant (without error), second, that it is necessary, in other words, that we cannot dispense with any part of it. Third, that it is sufficient, that it contains all that we need to know to be saved and live in a way that pleases God (we don't add extra bits). Fourth, that it is clear, it is not a code that needs cracking. Some parts are hard to understand, but mostly because our hearts are hard. Finally, we believe that Scripture is authoritative, it is the source that we turn to when we disagree.

WHY SHOULD I BELIEVE THAT THE BIBLE IS GOD'S WORD?

The short answer is because Jesus did. Jesus' teaching, as recorded in the gospels, is the central foundation of Christian doctrine and He repeatedly affirmed the place of the Old Testament in the life of God's people. He never questioned the contents or high importance of the Scriptures. Jesus also commissioned the New Testament, naming his apostles in the Gospels who wrote many of the letters. Jesus also added a later apostle, called Paul. Jesus personally appeared to him in Acts (Which is like the second part of the Gospel of Luke). Another apostle, Peter, also affirmed Paul's writings as Scripture in one of his letters.

WHAT ROLE SHOULD SCRIPTURE HAVE IN MY LIFE?

The Bible is a source of *knowledge*, it tells us things about God, how we should honour Him, things He has done and things He will do. It is also a source of *encouragement*, that God is on our side, mighty to save and sympathetic of our weaknesses. It is also a source of *correction*, challenging our stubbornness and selfish dispositions and helping us to live in the freedom of holiness. It is also a source of *direction*, it gives us our marching orders. Finally, it is a source of *wonder* that leads to praise as we learn about the awesome character of God.

HOW SHOULD I VIEW THE LAW IN THE OLD TESTAMENT?

One of the big questions that people have when they are reading the Bible is what role the Old Testament law has in the lives of Christians today. We will talk more about this in later sessions, but it is important to understand that the law was written for a certain people at a certain time in the history of redemption, that through the law they might be saved; Jesus has now fulfilled that law. The law therefore contains some moral standards that remain to this day (like not committing adultery) and all number of additional strict rules about what to wear, what to eat, and what sacrifices to make to pay the price for different sins. Christians are not bound by these fulfilled laws but recognize the important place the Old Testament has in informing us about the character of God and what life was like for God's people before Jesus.

IN WHAT ORDER SHOULD I READ THE BIBLE?

Most people find it helpful to start with some New Testament; reading one of the Gospels first and then some letters. In the Old Testament the poetry and history are often easier to understand than the law and the prophets. Though Genesis is categorized in the books of law, much of it is important history that is worth reading earlier on too.

"For the word of God is living and active, sharper than any two-edged sword" Hebrews 4:12

"The grass withers, the flower fades, but the word of our God will stand forever." Isaiah 40:8

"All Scripture is breathed out by God and profitable for teaching, for reproof, for correction, and for training in righteousness" 2 Timothy 3:16

"Your word is a lamp to my feet and a light to my path." Psalm 119:105

"Do not think that I have come to abolish the Law or the Prophets; I have not come to abolish them but to fulfill them." Matthew 5:17

YOUR QUESTIONS

Write out any questions you have from this session

- _____
- _____
- _____

STUDY QUESTIONS

What are the five sections of the Old Testament?

_____

_____

_____

What are the four gospels?

_____

_____

_____

What five qualities of the Bible have Christians historically believed in?

_____

_____

_____

PERSONAL REFLECTION QUESTIONS

How deeply do you trust the Bible and why?

_____

_____

_____

_____

_____

_____

What kind of bible reading schedule will best help you to grow as a Christian?

_____

_____

_____

_____

GROUP DISCUSSION QUESTIONS

Why do you think God has given us a book?

_____

_____

_____

_____

What is the meaning of Old Testament law for Christians today?

_____

_____

_____

_____

_____

How can we be sure that the Bible is reliable?

_____

_____

_____

_____

_____

SESSION II:
WHO IS GOD?

It has been said that the purpose of humanity is to glorify God by enjoying Him forever. Sin has created a distance between humanity and God and the most exciting thing about being a Christian is having a greater ability and passion to know your God in a deeply intimate and personal way.

WHAT ATTRIBUTES DOES HE HAVE?

Job 36:26 says "Behold, God is great, and we know him not". God's character is so vast and complex that we can never imagine that we know Him fully. Yet in Acts 17:27 it states that humanity's purpose is "that they should seek God, and perhaps feel their way toward him and find him". As such, there can never be a complete list of His attributes but we can find in Scripture much about who He is as we seek to feel our way towards Him.

BEING

Holy – God is sacred, He is set apart, enthroned as the Most High God above all other beings in importance. **Omnipotent** – He is all powerful, He can do all that He desires and is not limited in any way. **Omniscient** – His mind is infinite in knowledge, He is not parted from any item of truth in what is, was, will be and could be. **Omnipresent** – He is not bound by the dimension of space, He is present in His fullness in all places.

Eternal – He exists outside of time and is fully present in every moment of time as we experience it. **Majestic** – He is magnificently beautiful. **Unchanging** – He has never, and will never, change in any way. **Terrifying** – His presence is overwhelmingly and fearfully awesome. **Personal** – God is not a "force" but a conscious entity with a will, emotions and character.

WHERE IN THE BIBLE?

"Who is like you, O LORD...? Who is like you, majestic in holiness, awesome in glorious deeds, doing wonders?
Exodus 15:11

CHARACTER

JUSTICE

Just – God is perfect in fairness, eventually giving to each precisely what is deserved. **Righteous** – God's actions are morally perfect. **Loving** – God is perfect in adoring that which is adorable. **Wrathful** – God is perfect in despising that which is despicable. **Recompensing** – God is perfect in executing His passions. **Jealous** – God yearns for the glory that is His due.

"The Lord is a jealous and avenging God; ... and wrathful."
Nahum 1:2

GRACE

Generous – God is abundant in all His provisions, all things good come from Him and He gives to the undeserving. **Patient** – God does not dispense His vengeance as quickly as the wicked deserve. **Merciful** – God is sympathetic to the evil and gives relief to their suffering. **Faithful** – God is true to His word and to His character even where we are untrue to ours. **Forgiving** – God is ready to forgive His enemies. **Compassionate** – God is grieved at all suffering. **Caring** – the lives of humans matter to Him.

"a God merciful and gracious, slow to anger, and abounding in steadfast love and faithfulness ...forgiving iniquity"
Exodus 34:6

WHAT DOES IT MEAN THAT GOD IS A TRINITY?

THERE IS ONE GOD

It is important to understand that the universe has one being at its centre and that the purpose of all things is the glory of a single entity. There is a finality and uniqueness to this idea: that there is no one like God, no copies or equals; that He alone is worthy of praise and that our world is not run by a committee. We must take care not to picture God as being three persons who are merely similar or working in unison. God is not split up in any manner, He is absolutely singular.

HE EXISTS IN THREE PERSONS

God also has as a part of His eternal nature three distinct persons: The Father (who's will is sovereign over the Trinity), the Son (Jesus, the 'agent' of the Father's will) and the Holy Spirit (the presence of God perfecting and dwelling in the hearts of Christians). Each person is the same in being, character and worth, but different in function and in name. The persons speak to one another, glorify one another and love one another. We must take care not to imagine God as being like a person who has three jobs and simply switches from one to the others. He is, and always has been, three distinct persons.

EACH PERSON IS FULLY GOD

Each person of the Holy Trinity is in Himself the totality of God, not merely a part of God. God is not like a pie cut into three pieces. This is a very supernatural and complex concept, we do not encounter anything comparable on earth. There is not a contradiction here, i.e., we are not saying that a certain fact is true, but yet also false. Instead it is a paradox, i.e., a collection of facts that seem to be incompatible but actually are not.

WHAT DOES IT MEAN THAT GOD BECAME A MAN?

JESUS IS FULLY HUMAN

Jesus Christ was, and is, a full human person with all of the functions, emotions and common experiences that a person has. He has a human soul, mind and body. This is significant both in the sense that we have a saviour who can sympathize with us as an actual human and also that we can count Jesus as being a part of the human race, and able to stand as a representative of humanity before the Father. Jesus will be human forever and this doctrine is called the incarnation.

JESUS IS FULLY GOD

Even during His time on earth, Jesus was, and eternally will be, fully God. He did not give up anything of His divine nature when He became human. He was morally perfect, omniscient, omnipotent and holy. There are questions about what aspects of His divinity He 'laid aside' to assume this lowly role, and how His divine functions (for example His knowledge or omnipresence) were voluntarily held back, but at no point did He become anything other than God Almighty in His fullness.

"...The Lord our God, the Lord is one."
Deuteronomy 6:4

"...the Holy Spirit, whom the Father will send in my [Jesus'] name, he will teach you all things..."
John 14:26

"...to lie to the Holy Spirit... You have [lied] to God."
Acts 5:3-4

"Jesus is Lord"
Romans 10:9

"Now is my soul troubled"
John 12:27

"...a spirit does not have flesh and bones, as you see that I have"
Luke 24:39

"Thomas answered him, 'My Lord and my God!'"
John 20:28

YOUR QUESTIONS

Write out any questions you have from this session

- _____
- _____
- _____

STUDY QUESTIONS

List six attributes of God's nature

_____

_____

What are the three facts that make up the doctrine of the Trinity?

_____

_____

Describe the doctrine of the incarnation

_____

_____

PERSONAL REFLECTION QUESTIONS

What persuades you that God exists?

_____

_____

_____

_____

Which attribute of God do you find it hardest to accept? Why is this?

_____

_____

_____

_____

What does it mean for your relationship with God that He has become a man?

_____

_____

_____

_____

_____

GROUP DISCUSSION QUESTIONS

Which elements of God's character do you think are most absent from popular thinking about God?

_____

_____

_____

_____

_____

_____

Why is a belief in God as a trinity so important to Christianity?

_____

_____

_____

_____

_____

What is so wonderful about the incarnation?

_____

_____

_____

_____

_____

WHO AM I?

In addition to having new beliefs about God, becoming a Christian drastically changes the way you view yourself and the human community as a whole. In this session we will explore the biblical view of what it means to be human, created by God and yet to be a sinner, having rebelled against God and rejected His lordship.

HOW AM I MADE IN THE 'IMAGE OF GOD'?

God made humans 'in His own image'. This is an enormous part of understanding who we are. This means that all of the elements of God's character are found in humans to some degree, and that we are greatly valuable as a reflection of Him.

I AM MORAL
Animals are amoral, having no care for what is "right", but humans share God's sense of justice about what is right and wrong.

I AM RELATIONAL
We have been created to live in community. A person cannot function properly without healthy, inter-dependent community.

I AM SPIRITUAL
A person is the unity of a body and a spirit (or soul), our actions involve our spirit and though we are influenced by many things, we have free will to make our own choices and decide our own values and be responsible for them. Being spiritual also means having the ability to relate to, and have intimacy with, God.

WHAT DOES IT MEAN THAT I AM A SINNER?

Our perfect creation has been marred by sin. At the heart of sin is a disposition that God is not good and that we should instead meet our own needs at the expense of God's glory and the care of other people.

I AM IMMORAL
We do not primarily consider what is right anymore, sometimes having no care for what is good, other times purposely pursuing harm. We have become hurtful in our innermost being.

I AM SOLITARY
Sinners go through life mostly alone, being the only person ultimately concerned for our wellbeing and making most decisions based on our own pleasures.

I AM SECULAR
We are concerned with the immediate pleasures of the Earth rather than a relationship with the creator and giver of these things. We have rejected the higher form of being that we were; we are less God-like.

WHERE IN THE BIBLE?

"God created man in his own image"
Genesis 1:27

"...choose this day whom you will serve..."
Joshua 24:15

"It is not good that the man should be alone"
Genesis 2:18

"...every intention of the thoughts of [man's] heart was only evil continually"
Genesis 6:5

"...the stars are not pure in his eyes, how much less man, who is a maggot, the son of man, who is a worm!"
Job 25:5-6

WHERE DOES THAT LEAVE ME AS A CHRISTIAN?

For those who have repented of their sin and put their trust in the saving work of Jesus, sin is something being gradually removed from our hearts by the Holy Spirit, who dwells within us and helps us to make better choices day by day. We will not be perfect in this life and will continue to struggle with sin, but sin has now gone from being our friend to being our enemy – that means it is not something we are excited about or proud of, but something we mourn as we await the full removal of sin from our nature, which will happen when we die and are alive forever in heaven. Not only will we be free of sin but we will be glorified, like Christ, and in possession of His perfect righteousness. Our ability to make more righteous choices is a sign that we are truly saved.

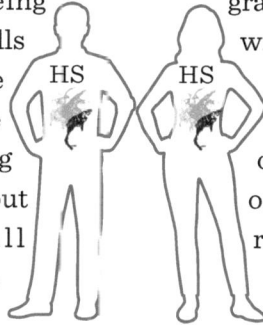

> "...your body is a temple of the Holy Spirit within you, whom you have from God? You are not your own, for you were bought with a price. So glorify God in your body"
> 1 Corinthians 6:19-20

ARE ALL PEOPLE DESERVING OF HELL?

Tragically, yes. On earth, humans are obviously a long way from perfect, but also a long way from how evil we would be if left to our own desires. Society creates many boundaries that hold back our true nature of sin and reward good behaviour. When societies break down, or cease to reward good behaviour, we see sin unmasked. Almost all of the police officers recruited to participate in the holocaust complied, we have to accept that many of us would have done the same thing in that situation. Also, God's grace is restraining the evil tendencies inside everyone. God gives His worst enemies the gifts of humility, goodness and love. The creature we would be in Hell would be our 'true' self, unrecognizable from who we are today. Finally, we as sinners ourselves are not fit to be the judge of what is deserved because we have become desensitized to how awful sin is and could never imagine how holy God really is. We must spin the question on its head: how holy would God have to be, and how awful would my true heart have to really be, that Hell would be a fair punishment for me?

> "God saw everything that he had made... it was very good"
> Genesis 1:31

> "Depart from me, you cursed, into the eternal fire"
> Matthew 25:41

DID GOD INTEND EVIL TO COME INTO THE WORLD?

Yes. God never committed any evil and any time someone sins they are always going against what pleases God. Though God is not pleased by evil, it does ultimately give Him glory to be contrasted against evil and to defeat it. Go through the attributes of God from session II and consider how many of them require the existence of evil in order to be demonstrated. Imagine God being worshiped for eternity and us never praising Him for His grace, mercy or justice. No person was ever forced against their will to sin, they chose to, but it is all in God's ultimate plan.

> "you meant evil against me, but God meant it for good"
> Genesis 50:20

HOW SHOULD I FEEL ABOUT MYSELF?

We should hold in balance the truth that we are redeemed and valued reflections of God and yet on the other hand still sinners. We should be thoroughly sorry for the life we have led, apologizing to people and repenting to God often but yet be in awe of how loved and dignified we are in Christ: children of God valued enough to die for. The Gospel should lead us on a journey that begins with sorrow but ends in Joy.

> "May the God of hope fill you with all joy"
> Romans 15:13

YOUR QUESTIONS

Write out any questions you have from this session

- _____

- _____

- _____

STUDY QUESTIONS

What does it mean that we are made in the image of God?

_____

_____

_____

How do you define sin?

_____

_____

_____

What relationship to sin do Christians experience in this life?

_____

_____

_____

PERSONAL REFLECTION QUESTIONS

Do you find it hard to accept that even people who have hurt you are made by God in His image? Why?

_____

_____

_____

_____

_____

_____

Do you find it hard to accept that you are personally responsible for your sin?

_____

_____

_____

_____

_____

In what ways have you seen the Holy Spirit begin to help you battle sin?

_____

_____

_____

_____

_____

GROUP DISCUSSION QUESTIONS

How can we explain to unbelievers what a high view of humanity we have?

_____

_____

_____

_____

How can we explain to unbelievers just how bad our sin really is?

_____

_____

_____

_____

How can we explain how the judgement of God is not unfair?

_____

_____

_____

_____

HOW AM I SAVED?

Having faced the supreme holiness of God and the awful depravity of human beings, we are led to the complex question of how a person is forgiven of their sin, reconciled to God and destined for eternity with Him in paradise. God, being both perfect in justice and abundant in grace, has devised an ingenious plan to execute both in perfection. The cross of Jesus Christ is at the heart of what Christianity is all about, without it, we have mere religion and philosophy, but with it we have eternal life.

HOW DID JESUS DIE FOR MY SIN?

Our sin has merited an eternal death penalty, incurred an infinite debt and has thoroughly wrecked our personal relationship with God, having turned it from love to wrath. The work of Jesus on the cross has accomplished salvation in each of these areas, thoroughly destroying the curse of sin. This doctrine is called the *atonement*.

SUBSTITUTION: JESUS TOOK THE DEATH PENALTY OF MY SIN.

The retributive justice of God requires that there is a direct consequence for sin in the form of an eternal death penalty. The spiritual agony of the cross was equal to the eternal agony due to the entire church in Hell.

SACRIFICE: JESUS PAID THE DEBT OF MY SIN.

This is the ultimate sense in which Jesus is the fulfillment of the Old Testament law. Under the law the greater your sin, the greater value your sacrifice had to be to atone for it. Jesus is a sacrifice of infinite value.

PROPITIATION: JESUS BORE THE WRATH OF GOD.

God is rightly angry at sin in a very direct and intense way. Jesus volunteers to be the one responsible for the sin of the church and thus invites the wrath of God to be spent on Him instead.

WHERE IN THE BIBLE?

"By his wounds you have been healed"
1 Peter 2:24

"we have been made holy through the sacrifice of the body of Jesus Christ"
Hebrews 10:10

"[God] loved us and sent his Son to be the propitiation for our sins."
1 John 4:10

"For our sake [God] made him [Jesus] to be sin who knew no sin, so that in him we might become the righteousness of God."
2 Corinthians 5:21

HOW IS IT FAIR FOR GOD TO PUNISH JESUS IN MY PLACE?

One of the starkest objections to the idea of the atonement is that it is unjust to punish and be angry at an innocent person and let the guilty go free. The answer to the objection is found in the union of Christ with the Church. Jesus, as a human, indeed as the "firstborn" of all creation, chose to become the head of this "new humanity" called the church. Another way this union is explained is as a marriage with Jesus as the husband. We inherit His righteousness and He inherits our sin. This union is so strong that God is satisfied to punish Jesus in our place.

HOW IS SALVATION APPLIED TO ME INTERNALLY?

Now that Jesus has been crucified, there is a way for sinners to be saved. There is then the process of that salvation being applied to an individual Christian:

REGENERATION

This means that the Holy Spirit wakes a person up from their spiritual sleep (or death) and turns them from being a persecutor of Jesus to a friend of Jesus, and from being a friend of sin to being an enemy of sin. It leaves a person open to accepting the gospel. Without the Spirit first working in us, we would not accept the gospel.

"he has caused us to be born again to a living hope"
1 Peter 1:3

ADOPTION

Becoming a Christian is to be adopted by the Father. Not everything that someone creates is their child, in the same way, though God created humans, He did not beget us as His children. Christians are adopted into the house of God.

"we are children of God, and if children, then heirs"
Romans 8:16-17

JUSTIFICATION

To be justified is to be declared innocent by God and not deserving of any punishment whatsoever. This is applied instantly to the believer because of what the Lord has done on the cross. This does not however make our actions instantly pure.

"There is... no condemnation for those... in Christ Jesus"
Romans 8:1

WHAT WILL BE DIFFERENT ABOUT ME EXTERNALLY?

We could ask: what can I do to be saved? The answer to this question is an emphatic "nothing". Faith, repentance and doing good works are not the deeds you must do to merit salvation, rather they are the mark of those who have become Christians.

REPENTANCE

A Christian will not feel the urge to defend their past actions as they once did. You will find yourself feeling a great degree of sorrow for the wrong you have done and will desire to repent often to God and to other people. Repentance is an essential part of becoming a Christian.

"repent and believe in the gospel"
Mark 1:15

FAITH

If repentance is turning your back on sin, faith is the simultaneous act of turning to Jesus alone for your salvation. Saving faith is not the act of believing something against the evidence, rather it is the simple act of trusting in the work of Christ to save us rather than our own works. There is nothing you can do to make God love you more, and nothing you can do to make God love you less.

"one is justified by faith apart from works of the law"
Romans 3:28

SANCTIFICATION

Throughout your life as a Christian, you will notice that the pull of sin is weaker and the enticement of goodness is stronger. Though never perfect in this life, our actions gradually become more righteous and our sensitivity to sin becomes more acute.

"by... one man's obedience the many will be made righteous"
Romans 5:19

YOUR QUESTIONS

Write out any questions you have from this session

- _____

- _____

- _____

STUDY QUESTIONS

What are the three aspects of the atonement?

_____

_____

_____

What are three ways that salvation is applied internally to a person?

_____

_____

_____

What are the three external signs of salvation?

_____

_____

_____

PERSONAL REFLECTION QUESTIONS

What encourages you about the atonement?

_____

_____

_____

_____

_____

_____

_____

Do you feel as though you can pinpoint when you were regenerated?

_____

_____

_____

_____

_____

What encourages you about the doctrine of adoption?

_____

_____

_____

_____

_____

GROUP DISCUSSION QUESTIONS

Why is the atonement the only way that a sinner can be forgiven?

_____

_____

_____

_____

How can we know if a person has been saved?

_____

_____

_____

_____

What is the relationship of good works to salvation?

_____

_____

_____

_____

SESSION V:

WHAT IS THE CHURCH?

We have understood the basic message of the Bible: that sinners can be reconciled to a holy God through the cross of Christ. What do we call this group of saved people? We are called the Church, and in this session we will explore what that means.

WHAT KIND OF PEOPLE HAVE I BECOME A PART OF?

It has eternally been in the saving plan of God to carve out a people for Himself who can be separate from "Adam's race" and be a new humanity that will be freed from the curse of sin. This began with Abraham. Abraham was the first Jew and from His offspring came all the Israelites, a people set apart for God. Jesus came by the Jews (being an ancestor of Abraham) to fulfill the promise of salvation for the Jews. When Jesus ascended into heaven and sent His Holy Spirit, we as believing non-Jews (Gentiles) were grafted on to the remaining faithful Jews and we are now all known as 'the Church'. There is an important sense in which it is not each person individually who is saved, but we as a collective group.

WHAT DOES THE CHURCH DO?

The Church is not a club for Christians, we are an invasive force in a strange and foreign world that is actually the home and the natural habitat of sin. The Gospel is not an institution to be defended, it is a weapon to be wielded. It is a piece of news – that a holy God has been crucified for our sin – that has the power to destroy the grip of sin. We do not long remain on this Earth, we are dying and we live among a people who are dying. The Church is above all else a missional community, we exist to participate in the work of Jesus in reconciling Man to God, both in sharing the good news of salvation and helping it to work itself out in believers such that we may be even more effective in our witness of Jesus. Many do this where they are, others are sent to foreign lands.

HOW SHOULD IT BE GOVERNED & WHY SO MANY KINDS?

When the Church began in the first century, the Apostles governed the whole Church. Even among them, there was no leader and each church had its own leadership. In the centuries that followed, leadership became more centralized. Although the Church was originally made up of lowly Jewish converts (many women and slaves) who were often persecuted, more non-Jews became Christians and eventually, in 312 ad, even the emperor of Rome, Constantine, became a Christian. Christianity thus became mainstream in the west.

Unfortunately, too much emphasis was placed on the authority of the leaders and less on the Bible. The church grew stale and its doctrine became weak, teaching that sinners are saved by good deeds rather than by Jesus' free gift of grace. In 1517, a reformation began and the church became split between Catholics and Protestants. Protestant churches make God's word, not the Pope, the final authority and are normally governed mainly by their own leaders, called elders, and a pastor(s) who lead the church vocationally. Elders are normally elected by people who have become members of their church. The Bible calls us to submit to our elders.

WHERE IN THE BIBLE?

"...salvation is from the Jews." John 4:22

"it is those of faith who are the sons of Abraham." Galatians 3:7

"I am not ashamed of the gospel, for it is the power of God for salvation to everyone who believes" Romans 1:16

"Go therefore and make disciples of all nations" Matthew 28:19

WHAT IS THE PURPOSE OF A CHURCH SERVICE?

To glorify God by proclaiming the gospel. It is worked out in believers and unbelievers alike. These are some of the things we do on Sunday to achieve this:

PREACHING

The gospel is preached in a sermon. It is spoken with authority, clarity and passion. The church is led from behind the pulpit, it is the kind of helm of the church. The preacher will take a passage of Scripture and unpack it for the congregation. It will involve some encouragement, some rebuke, some information and some application and many other things. We should be eager to listen carefully to a sermon and believe that God has something profound to say to us each time we listen to a sermon– if we find a sermon boring or irrelevant, it is up to us to work harder to understand what God is saying to us through the passage of Scripture.

FELLOWSHIP & PRAYER

The gospel is also made real to us as we gather together and share fellowship. Caring for one another happens both in the service and throughout the week. Our most visible distinctive is that we love one another and this preaches the gospel through loud actions, both to one another and to non-believers as they witness our love for one another. Other Christians are not merely our neighbours they are our brothers and sisters. Our fellowship also includes fellowship with God through prayer.

THE LORD'S SUPPER

Also called communion, this symbol demonstrates the truth of the gospel by taking a piece of bread that symbolizes Jesus' body, broken for us and a taking a sip of wine that symbolizes His blood, shed for us. This is done regularly by believers to constantly remind us of Jesus' sacrifice and to taste the riches of His delicious grace.

SINGING

Humanity has always connected and expressed its deepest feelings with music. Melodies can convey emotion in ways that words cannot and music is therefore a gift from God that we give back to Him by singing His praises. There is something powerful about coming together as a people and proclaiming the glory of God and the truth about Him in chorus, with one voice, in the form of song.

BAPTISM

When a person becomes a Christian, we baptize (literally: "immerse") them in water and raise them back up to symbolize their own death to sin and resurrection to a new life in Jesus. This is done once publicly to proclaim that person's salvation. This is yet another public proclamation of the gospel.

GIVING

We live out the gospel through giving. 100% of our income belongs to God, we are merely taking care of it and spending it on His behalf. How would God desire it to be spent? He would want us to take care of ourselves and our family, He would also want us to give money to further the gospel cause: Traditionally, many Christians have given a tenth of their income to the church.

"preach the word... reprove, rebuke, and exhort"
2 Timothy 4:2

"...eat this bread and drink the cup, you proclaim the Lord's death..."
1 Corinthians 11:26

"Oh come, let us sing to the Lord"
Psalm 95:1

"God loves a cheerful giver" 2 Corinthians 9:7

"Repent and be baptized every one of you"
Acts 2:38

"Above all, keep loving one another earnestly,"
1 Peter 4:8

YOUR QUESTIONS

Write out any questions you have from this session

- _____

- _____

- _____

STUDY QUESTIONS

How do you define "the Church"?

_____

_____

_____

How do you define the mission of the Church?

_____

_____

_____

Name three elements of a Church service and their purpose

_____

_____

PERSONAL REFLECTION QUESTIONS

What did you learn about the purpose and definition of the church in this session?

_____

_____

_____

_____

_____

_____

Which element of your church's service do you most look forward to and why?

_____

_____

_____

_____

Which element of your church's service do you least look forward to and why?

_____

_____

_____

_____

GROUP DISCUSSION QUESTIONS

Why is it important that the Church is missional?

_____

_____

_____

_____

Is it a bad thing that there are many different denominations?

_____

_____

_____

_____

What makes for a good sermon?

_____

_____

_____

_____

SESSION VI:

WHAT SHOULD I DO?

We have covered what it means to be and do Church, (in a sense the question: what do we do?) but in addition to being a community of believers, we are also individual Christians that must grow as disciples of Jesus. Becoming a Christian involves ceasing to sin (which is our next session: what do I not do?) but it also involves starting to live in the Spirit.

WHAT KIND OF CHARACTER SHOULD I NOW HAVE?

Our character is made new in Christ. In Galatians 5:22-23 we have listed the 'fruits of the Spirit'. These are a guide for us in recognizing the work of Spirit within us.

FRUITS OF THE SPIRIT:

Love – We should feel compassion for others, learning to like them

Joy – Following Jesus is not about being perpetually gleeful, but knowing God does come with a deep sense of joy even through tears and suffering

Peace – The Christian is not in turmoil being frustrated with life, but rests in the truth that God is in control and that He will judge all things

Patience – We should be able to wait well without a presumption that the world revolves around us and our timing

Kindness – A Christian is generous with their time, money and words.

Goodness – We take delight in living righteously

Faithfulness – Christians keep their word, to others and to God.

Gentleness – We do not want to be needlessly aggressive or harsh, but speak and act with grace, generosity and approachability

Self-control – We are no longer controlled by our animalistic urges, but by our deeper desire to honour God

> **WHERE IN THE BIBLE?**
>
> **"walk by the Spirit, and you will not gratify the desires of the flesh. For the desires of the flesh are against the Spirit, and the desires of the Spirit are against the flesh"**
> Galatians 5:16-17

HOW DOES GOD GIFT INDIVIDUAL CHRISTIANS?

GIFTS OF THE SPIRIT:

Teaching – Not many are gifted to be teachers in the Church. We should be hesitant to assume we have this gift – see if it is confirmed by others

Prophesying – We believe God speaks today by prophetically implanting knowledge into the minds of believers, but we are very careful to test both the reputation of the prophet and the content of the prophecy against Scripture, reason, and reality.

Encouraging – One of the most under-rated gifts, encouragers build up the church with words of hope and life.

Wisdom – Knowing how to apply truth in a godly way

Evangelism – All are called to evangelize, but some are especially gifted

Healing – We believe God heals miraculously and some people have a particular gift to pray for God's physical healing. We must be careful that this is not used in place of medicine – which is another of God's gifts. We are also careful not to praise the one who has the gift.

Administration – The ability to manage many tasks and get them done

Discernment – To tell the difference between what is good and evil.

Mercy – Caring about the suffering and providing relief to the hurting

> **"there are varieties of gifts, but the same Spirit... To each is given... for the common good."**
> 1 Corinthians 12:4-7
>
> **"As each has received a gift, use it to serve one another... in everything God may be glorified."**
> 1 Peter 4:10-11

There is no comprehensive list of the spiritual gifts in the Bible, the above list is just a collection of some. The Bible tells us to eagerly desire the gifts of the Spirit so that we might be a blessing to the church and a witness to the world. We should seek to identify what gifts we have and allow other Christians to confirm that we do indeed have the gifts that we think we do. In this way, everyone in the Church has something to contribute

HOW AND WHY SHOULD I PRAY?

Despite the work of the Spirit, our character and our gifts are weak compared to how broken the world is and how great our task is. Those who live in the Spirit are therefore drawn to prayer. When we pray, we are not doing God a service, we are falling at His feet and crying out to Him. The four parts of Christian prayer are sometimes described in the acronym ACTS: Adoration = praising God for who He is. Confession = repenting deeply and specifically for our sin. Thanksgiving = pouring out our heart of appreciation for His generosity Supplication = asking God for things we need Him to do for us.

We pray because we are weak and God is strong. Jesus says that whatever we ask in His name we will receive, so why do we often feel like prayer is unanswered? It is because our definition of prayer is faulty. Prayer is petitioning God:

PERSISTENTLY

God, in his wisdom, knows not just what we need, but when we need it. Prayer that asks once for something and then gives up is not really done in faith or authentically. We must wrestle with God in prayer, showing patience and commitment.

AUTHENTICALLY

Authenticity in prayer means three things. First, that we are humble. Humility is nothing more than facing up to the reality of your situation. In Luke 18:13 Jesus says the humble tax collector "would not even lift up his eyes to heaven, but beat his breast, saying, 'God be merciful to me, a sinner!' I tell you, this man went down to his house justified". Second, it means praying earnestly; prayer must be the real you, praying to the real God. Third, it means confessing sin. We cannot waltz up to the throne of God if we are in a pattern of unrepentant sin, we must first be sorry.

IN FAITH

Prayer that is faithless is insulting to God, it is as though there is some merit in simply speaking out words to God even if He isn't really hearing them or really bothered by them or mighty enough to answer the prayer. We must come to God expecting that He will answer, even if it is not in the way we hope.

IN ACCORDANCE WITH GOD'S WILL

God is our Father, if we ask for something good, He will not give us something bad. In fact, when we ask for something bad, we will still be given that which is good. Another way of phrasing that is that God will give us even greater gifts than we know how to ask for. In reality this can greatly dishearten us because we are often mistaken about what it is that is good for us. We often desire immediate relief from suffering that God has ordained for our benefit, or we seek worldly goods that would spoil us instead of spiritual growth.

"You do not have, because you do not ask."
James 4 2

"believe that you have received it, and it will be yours."
Mark 11:24

"God opposes the proud but gives grace to the humble."
1 Peter 5 5

"all night [Jesus] continued in prayer to God."
Luke 6:12

"if we ask anything according to his will he hears us."
1 John 5:14

YOUR QUESTIONS

Write out any questions you have from this session

- _____

- _____

- _____

STUDY QUESTIONS

Name three fruits of the Spirit:

_____

_____

_____

Name three gifts of the Spirit:

_____

_____

_____

What are the four qualities of Biblical prayer?

_____

_____

_____

PERSONAL REFLECTION QUESTIONS

What fruits of the Spirit do you see growing in your heart recently?

_____

_____

_____

_____

_____

_____

How do you feel that you have been gifted to serve the Church?

_____

_____

_____

_____

_____

Which of the four qualities of Biblical prayer do you feel your prayers lack?

_____

_____

_____

_____

_____

GROUP DISCUSSION QUESTIONS

Which fruit of the Spirit do you think is most needed in our world today?

_____

_____

_____

_____

Share with the group how God has used you in your gifts

_____

_____

_____

_____

What other qualities are important in sustaining a healthy prayer life?

_____

_____

_____

_____

SESSION VII:

WHAT DO I NOT DO?

In the previous two sessions we have covered some of the main changes that occur when you become a follower of Jesus, both in community as the Church and as an individual. We are now looking at what it is that we have left behind, namely sin. Abandoning sin brings new life in very specific, personal ways. Sin is always a matter of the heart that spills into our actions, but let us look at how sin manifests itself in how we act.

WHAT CHANGES ABOUT THE USE OF MY MIND?

Pride ➡ Humility.
Christians should not be obsessed with themselves. Being humble is as simple counting others as more significant than yourself and not placing your sense of worth in your capabilities.

Envy ➡ Thankfulness.
Christians should not covet the possessions and circumstances of their neighbour in a spiteful way, we should be filled with joy when our friends are blessed.

Unforgiveness ➡ Forgiveness.
We have been forgiven much that we might in turn forgive all who ask forgiveness from us; it would be utter hypocrisy to do otherwise. Forgiveness and mercy are hallmarks of good Christian character.

WHAT CHANGES ABOUT THE USE OF MY TONGUE?

Slander ➡ Encouragement.
Speaking nasty words about someone else is embarrassing because it reflects a desperate need to appear holier than others. It shows great character to build each other up in encouragement.

Judgement ➡ Acceptance.
We are not to confuse having a boldness in privately convicting a person over their sin (as a means to help them back to freedom) with playing the judge. To judge is to gleefully condemn someone either for their choices or for their sin. It stems not from a righteous hatred of evil but from looking for an excuse to puff yourself up as though you are not also a sinner.

Lying ➡ Honesty.
To deceive others removes our ability to be trusted and respected in our community, it takes a long time to regain people's trust when you are known to lie. Christians should have a reputation for honesty, even when the temptation to lie is compelling.

WHAT CHANGES ABOUT THE USE OF MY HANDS?

Anger ➡ Peace.
Anger, like all evil, begins in the heart, but the end result is acts of violence or other nastiness against others. Christians should not allow hatred of others in our heart, we should be people of peace, grieved by the pain of others.

WHERE IN THE BIBLE?

"When pride comes, then comes disgrace" Proverbs 11:2

"...love does not envy" 1 Corinthians 13:4

"if he sins... saying, 'I repent,' you must forgive him." Luke 17:4

"...whoever utters slander is a fool." Proverbs 10:18

"who are you to judge your neighbour?" James 4:12

"You shall not bear false witness." Exodus 20:16

"Vengeance is mine... says the Lord." Romans 12:19

Greed ➡ Generosity.

Christians should not strive for our own gain, rather we should strive for the wellbeing of others. Greed brings bitterness and misery.

Theft ➡ Hard Work.

To steal is to benefit from someone else's labour without their permission. If someone makes something, or owns something, we are to treat that with respect. If we are lacking anything, we should work hard to obtain it with our own labour realizing that we are owed nothing by the world.

WHAT CHANGES ABOUT THE USE OF MY SEXUALITY?

At the heart of sexual immorality is the disposition of taking animalistic pleasure (the stimulation of our bodies) at the disregard of the emotional damage we are doing to ourselves and others as a result.

Pornography ➡ Wholesomeness.

Pornography isharmful because it promotes a view of others as being mere objects for our lust. All of the women (and men) depicted in pornography are real people with their own struggles, feelings, and eternal destinations. A compassionate love for one's neighbour does not produce a desire to strip them bare and gawk at their body, removing their dignity and sense of personhood, even if they consent. Looking at pornography trains your brain to think of strangers as being sex objects to serve you and provide stimulation on demand. It also creates a desire for greater and greater novelty and shock value, and it is the starting point of all kinds of sexual sin and even extreme sexual crimes like rape and pædophilia. It also unfairly raises expectations of sex in marriage. Pornography can also include sexual fantasies that you conjure up in your head. If you are being stimulated by the imagined nakedness of someone, it is without their consent and is wrong for all the reasons that pornography is wrong.

Fornication ➡ Respect.

The word fornication means behaving sexually outside of marriage. Sex is an expression of passion unparalleled by any other act. Sex gives us the potential to love someone greatly, or to hurt them deeply. When we engage in sexual acts outside of the covenant of marriage, we are hurting, not helping, that person because in sex you give so deeply of yourself and in such a personal way that to engage in it with a mere pre-marital partner is to diminish the value of their personhood and make them feel cheapened. Women are often the victims of this and the assumption of many women is that all men are unavoidably desiring them mainly for their body and secondarily for their heart, Christian men can show women the difference Christ makes in the heart of a man by respecting women's bodies.

Adultery ➡ Faithfulness.

Adultery is obviously an awful thing to experience, especially for the victim, but also for those who have to bear the guilt of having committed it. Faithfulness means making your entire sexual gratification the exclusive domain of your spouse – this means what you think about, look at and desire. It also means persevering in your marriage no matter how tough things get. Divorce is one of the most painful things you can do to your spouse and children and so Christians must avoid it at all costs. Ask your group leader about how this may apply to your situation if this is something personal to you.

> "A greedy man stirs up strife"
> Proverbs 28:25

> "The labourer deserves his wages."
> 1 Timothy 5:18

> "everyone who looks at a woman with lustful intent has already committed adultery with her in his heart."
> Matthew 5:28

> "Put to death... sexual immorality, impurity..."
> Colossians 3:5

> "[treat] younger women as sisters, in all purity."
> 1 Timothy 5:2

> "Everyone who divorces his wife and marries another commits adultery, and he who marries a woman divorced from her husband commits adultery."
> Luke 16:18

29

YOUR QUESTIONS

Write out any questions you have from this session

- _____
- _____
- _____

STUDY QUESTIONS

Name something about the use of your mind that should change?

_____

_____

_____

Name something about the use of your tongue that should change?

_____

_____

_____

Name something about the use of your hands that should change?

_____

_____

_____

PERSONAL REFLECTION QUESTIONS

Which of the four areas (mind, tongue, hands, sexuality) do you find to be most difficult right now?

_____

_____

_____

_____

_____

Which of the four areas have you experienced the most growth in your life?

_____

_____

_____

_____

_____

What concrete steps can you take to make improvements in these areas?

_____

_____

_____

_____

_____

GROUP DISCUSSION QUESTIONS

Which of the twelve points do you think is the biggest issue for our society?

_____

_____

_____

_____

How can the church help people in the community to overcome sin?

_____

_____

_____

_____

How have you personally been able to see improvement in these areas of sin?

_____

_____

_____

_____

www.ingramcontent.com/pod-product-compliance
Lightning Source LLC
Chambersburg PA
CBHW042057040426
42447CB00003B/264

9 780986 960727